Speech In Motion

Speech In Motion

Sign Language Workbook 1

Marian Berry

To order additional copies of this book, contact:
Xlibris LLC
1-888-795-4274
www.Xlibris.com
Orders@Xlibris.com
551498

SPEECH IN MOTION

Hello and welcome to **SPEECH IN MOTION**. This self study workbook is to help you on your way to mastering the skills needed for communicating in sign language.

REMEMBER

"Don't listen with your ears"
" LISTEN WITH YOUR EYES"

Thank you to all who helped in any way in the past and in the continuing transition of this workbook.

Destiny Berry, Bonita Johnson-Gorin, Janet Lloyd Massey, Joshua Osborn, Greg Ruiz, and Araceli Zurita Osborn

PLEDGE OF ALLEGIANCE

I pledge (promise) allegiance (support) to the flag of the United States of America, and to the Republic for which it stands (represents), one Nation under God, indivisible with liberty and justice for all.

Pledge of Allegiance

Pledge (promise) Allegiance (support)

Flag

United

States

America

Republic

Which

Stands

One

Nation

Under

God

Indivisible

Liberty

Justice

For

All

TABLE OF CONTENTS

Culture / Language Notes 1

Terminology 3

Relative Positing 5

More Information on How Signs are Made 7

Finger Spelling 12

Words You Are Interested In Learning 13

Vocabulary Words 15

Vocabulary Words 17

Manual Alphabet 18

Finger Spelling Practice 20

Numbers 21

Syntax 28

Lesson 1 29
    Vocabulary Words

    Practice Sentences

    Short Story—"All About Amy"

    Name That Sign

Lesson 2 39
    Vocabulary Words

    Practice Sentences

    Short Story—"Sara's Family"

    Name That Sign

Lesson 3 47

    Vocabulary Words

    Practice Sentences

    Short Story—"Grandma And Grandpa"

    Name That Sign

Lesson 4 59

    Vocabulary Words

    Practice Sentences

    Short Story—"Trouble With The Toilet"

    Name That Sign

Lesson 5 67

    Vocabulary Words

    Practice Sentences

    Name That Sign

Lesson 6 75

    Vocabulary Words

    Practice Sentences

    Short Story (5 & 6)—"Choosing Colors"

    Name That Sign

Answers 93

    Vocabulary Word Search Lesson 1

    Vocabulary Word Search Lesson 2

    Vocabulary Word Search Lesson 5

    Name That Sign

    Lesson 6 Test Answers

Vocabulary Word Pictures Lessons 1 thru 6 101

CULTURE / LANGUAGE NOTES

Introduction to
American Sign Language

Many people mistakenly believe that American Sign Language (ASL) is English conveyed through signs. Some think that it is a manual code for English that can express only concrete information or that there is one universal sign language used by Deaf people around the world.

Linguistic research demonstrates, however, that ASL, is comparable in complexity and expressiveness to spoken languages. It is not a form of English; it has its own distinct grammatical structure, which must be mastered in the same way as the grammar of any other language. ASL differs from spoken languages in that it is visual rather than auditory, and is composed of precise hand shapes and movements.

ASL is not universal. Just as hearing people in different countries speak different languages, so do deaf people around the world sign different languages. Because of historical circumstances, contemporary ASL is more like French Sign Language than like British Sign Language.

ASL was developed by American Deaf people to communicate with each other and has existed as long as there have been deaf Americans. Standardization was begun in 1817, when Laurent Clerc and Thomas H. Gallaudet established the first School for the Deaf in the U.S. Students afterwards spread the use of ASL to other parts of the U.S. and Canada. Traditionally, the language has been passed from one generation to the next in the residential school environment, especially through dormitory life. Even when signs were not permitted in the classroom, the children of

Deaf parents, as well as Deaf teachers and staff , would secretly pass on the language to other students. ASL is now used by approximately one-half million Deaf people in the U.S., and Canada. It is now the 4th most used language in the world. It is just behind German.

Since the late 1800's, Deaf people have been discouraged from using ASL. Many well-meaning, but misguided educators, believing that the only way for deaf people to fit into the hearing world is through speech and lip-reading, have insisted that deaf children try to learn to speak English. Some have even gone so far as to tie down deaf children's hands to prevent them from signing. Despite these and other attempts to discourage signing, ASL continues to be the preferred language of the Deaf Community. Far from seeing the use of sign as a handicap, the Deaf regard ASL as their natural language which reflects their cultural values and keeps their traditions and heritage alive.

TERMINOLOGY

FINGER SPELLING: A manual alphabet to form words and sentences.

MANUAL ALPHABET: The 26 different finger and hand positions representing the alphabet.

EXPRESSIVE SKILL: To be able to express yourself in sign language and finger spelling.

RECEPTIVE SKILL: To be able to receive and understand what is expressed in both finger-spelling and in signs.

ASL (American Sign Language)   A visual gestured language used by deaf persons in America.
It is based on concept.

CONCEPTUAL SIGNING: Choosing to use a sign based on the concept being expressed and and not the equivalent English word.

PSE (Pidgen Sign English):   Referring to signing that combines the grammatical structure of English and the signs of ASL. PSE gives you the ability to move on a pendulum from one form of signing to another.

SEE SIGN (Signing Exact English)   Signing every word.

ICONIC: Signs that look like an aspect of its
                                 referent.

Airplane, Airport

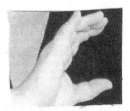

House
Shape of House

Airplane
Fly

Police
Wears Badge

NON-MANUAL CUE: A facial expression or other body
                                 language that contributes to the
                                 meaning of a sign.

RELATIVE POSITING

SIGNING SPACE: Your signing space is from the top of your head to your waist and from shoulder to shoulder. The hands are in front of the chest just about chin level.

Signing Space

HAND POSITION: Relaxing the hand turn your palm to face out between a 10:00 and 12:00 o'clock position.

FINGER SPELLING: Should be smooth without bouncing or jerking the arm or the hand.

VISUAL FOCUS: Eyes are not focused on the hands. You should be able to see the facial expression as well as the hands.

DOMINANT HAND: The signers preferred hand left or right.

SYMMETRY: Many signs use two hands moving independently of each other. They almost always have the same hand shape, location, and type of movement.

THE SIGNS:

ic hand shapes in forming signs. What the sign means

1. Hand shape
2. Orientation
3. Location
4. Movement

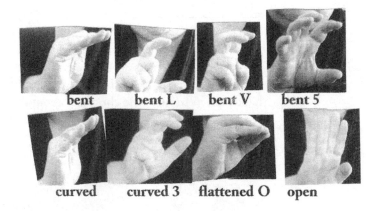

bent   bent L   bent V   bent 5

curved   curved 3   flattened O   open

MORE INFORMATION
ON HOW SIGNS ARE MADE

In ASL and PSE there are no tenses. There are no articles like "the." There is no sign for the word "be." The sign "true," is used in place of be. To let a person know if they are talking about the past, present, or future a time reference is used. This is an imaginary time line that places the person in the present and any signs made going in a downward motion are for the present time, everything happening in front of the body with a forward movement is the future and signs made going toward the back of the person are in the past.

TIME LINE

PAST   **NOW**   **FUTURE**

To begin, we know that things change as time goes on. That is how it is with signs, they evolve to make it easier to sign. Many signs that were made with two hands are now made with one hand. Take for example the sign for cow. There was a time when the sign was made with two hands and now it is made with one.

7

Cow (two hands)   **Cow**

There are some signs that begin with one hand shape and end with another. The sign for pretty begins with the open 5 hand and ends with the flattened O shape or as some like to call it the "and" hand.

Pretty   **Sleep**

POSSESSIVE PRONOUNS

These pronouns are done with the open hand. If the object belongs to you then the palm of the open hand faces you. If the object belongs to another person then the palm of the hand faces that person.

Ex.: mine, yours

My, Mine   **His, Hers, Its**

PERSONAL PRONOUNS

These pronouns are done the same way as with possessive pronouns only you use the index finger instead of the open hand. (Pointing toward you or to the other person).

SPATIAL SIGNING

In signing there is never a problem with pointing to a person who is not there. You use the appropriate sign and give that sign a place. Ex.: If I said that the book is not mine it is HIS. I would point to a place and that place would become representative of the person I am speaking about. Every time I speak of that person I would point to the same place.

REFLECTIVE PRONOUNS

If the word I am using is meant to mean for more than one person, I use the same sign, but I will a sweeping motion while doing the sign.

Ex.: you

Yours

FACIAL EXPRESSIONS

When signing, it is very important to use the appropriate facial expression to go along with the meaning of the sign. If you do not you could be sending a double message. You would not want to sign the word "happy," and have a sad look on your face.

MALE AND FEMALE

Signs that refer to a male or a female are done by location. Male nouns are usually done near the forehead and female signs are done near the cheek or chin.

Ex:

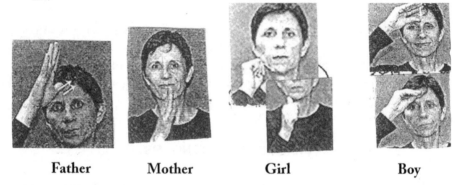

| Father | Mother | Girl | Boy |

PERSON ENDING

To transform a word to a person's occupation we put a person ending on the sign. As in the word "teach" we add the person ending and get "teacher."

Person marker   Person

Classifier:

A classifier is a hand shape that is used to represent an object. It can be a person or a thing. It will be made in a way to represent its size or shape. It can be used to show the place, movement, or how many there are.

Ex.: One car behind another

One car following another

Two cars

Two cars

Noun/Verb:

When there are two words that use the same basic signs, as in the words "food" and "eat, " the sign for "food" is done twice and the sign for "eat" is done once. In other words the noun has a double movement and the verb a single or no movement.

Ex.:

Food

Eat

Chair, seat

Sit

Finger Spelling

What is finger spelling? Finger spelling is the process of spelling out words by using signs that correspond to the letters of the word. (Manual Alphabet). There are 22 handshapes that, when held in certain positions and/or are produced with certain movements, represent the letters of the American alphabet.

When do you fingerspell? The most common uses are for names of people, places, movies, books, brand names, and when you do not know the sign for a word. Sometimes a word will be finger spelled because it is just as fast or faster to spell it. Example: C-A-R.

There are two finger spelled letters that trace their shape in the air: "Z" and "J."

In general your palm faces 10 o'clock. If it hurts to hold your hand in a certain position DON'T DO IT. Just hold your hand up in a comfortable position with the palm facing mostly forward.

"G" and "Q" use the same handshape. The "Q" is palm down.
"K" and "P" use the same handshape. The "P" is palm down. The "K" is palm forward.
"I" and "J" use the same handshape. The "J" traces a "J" in the air.
"H" and "U" use the same handshape. The "H" is horizontal. The "U" is vertical.

Note: Warm up hands and fingers to avoid injury before beginning to sign by opening and closing hands.

WORDS YOU ARE INTERESTED IN LEARNING

Vocabulary Words

LESSON 1	LESSON 2	LESSON 3	LESSON 4
ABC'S	ASK/QUESTION	ALL	ANGRY/MAD
AGAIN	AUNT/UNCLE	AND	BATHROOM/TOILET
DEAF/HEARING	BABY	BIG/SMALL	CHILDREN/CHILD
HOW	BOOK	CAN/CAN'T	COMPUTER
LOVE	BOY/GIRL	COME/GO	FEEL
MEET	BROTHER/SISTER	ENOUGH/FULL	FINE
MISUNDERSTAND	FAMILY	FRIEND	FOOD/EAT
NAME	FATHER/MOTHER	GRANDMA/GRANDPA	HERE
NICE/CLEAN	FINISH/START	HELP	HOME
PAST/FUTURE	GOOD/BAD	LIKE	HOUR/TIME
PLEASE/SORRY	HAPPY/SAD	LIVE	HOUSE
SIGN	HAVE	MARRY/DIVORCE	MILK
SLOW/FAST	MAN/WOMAN	NEED	MONTH
SPELL/FINGERSPELL	ME/YOU	NUMBER 1-23	MORNING/NIGHT
STUDENT	MEAN	OUT/IN	NOW
TEACHER	MY/MINE/YOUR	PERSON/PEOPLE	OLD/NEW

THANK YOU	NO/DON'T	RIGHT/WRONG	SIT/STAND
UNDERSTAND	OPEN/CLOSE	SAME/DIFFERENT/BUT	STAY/LEAVE
WHAT	REMEMBER/FORGET	SCHOOL	TREE
WHEN	SON/DAUGHTER	SEE	WATER
WHERE	TODAY/TOMORROW	THAT/THIS	WEEK
WHO	WE/US	THINK/HOW	YESTERDAY
WHY	WORK	WORD	
		YES/NO	

VOCABULARY WORDS

LESSON 5	LESSON 6
ANY / OTHER	BEFORE / AFTER
BED / SLEEP	COAT
BLACK / WHITE	COFFEE / TEA
BLUE	DO
BROWN	DOG / CAT / BIRD
COLOR	FLOWER
DRINK	FOR
DRIVE	GET
EXCUSE	GIVE
GOLD	HAPPEN
GREEN	LIGHT / DARK
MAKE	LISTEN
MOVE / PUT / WAIT	NEAR / FAR
ORANGE	NUMBERS 24-100, 1000, 1,000,000
PHONE	READY
PINK	SOCKS∧ /SHOES
PURPLE	TALL /SMALL
RED	TRY
SHOP / STORE	WANT / DON'T WANT
SILVER	WITH / WITHOUT
TALK	
WAIT	

Manual Alphabet

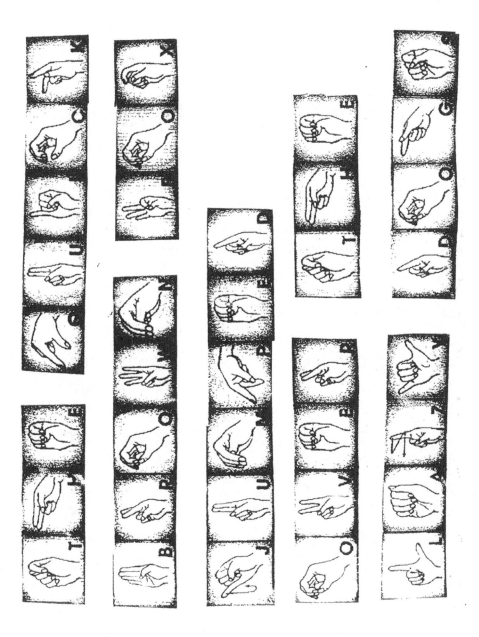

FINGER SPELLING PRACTICE

Time yourself for one (1) minute finger spelling each of the words. After the minute is up count **each letter.** Write the total down. Do this three (3) times. Then add all three totals and divide by three (3). This will give you an idea of how many characters you are doing per minute.

ALL	NAP	JET	EEL	QUIT	INK
ELF	ABD	ECHO	LAB	GAB	FACT
QUILL	NAB	ADD	QUAD	GEM	HIGH
ECU	FAD	BAD	HAG	FONT	HAM
KIN	PAN	LED	LEG	DIG	JOT
BUT	JUG	ILL	CAP	MAP	POX
BEG	GIG	OFF	DUB	KEEP	OATH
OBIT	ICON	PUN	HOT	DOG	BOY
MUTT	CUT	PIG	KNOW	KNOB	OOPS
EWE	ICE	GALE	JAM	JUMP	JAW
JERK	RAG	RAW	HOP	EAST	AND
ARE	ACHE	JAR	CAR	FAR	CAT
EAR	EVE	LAW	KNIT	COW	HOW
EBB	JAG	FOOT	QUEEN	BUD	COP
PAM	CAN	MAN	EAT	BIG	LID
FOX	DIS	MOM	OLD	NEW	BIN

NUMBERS

Numbers 1 Thru 9

ONE

TWO

THREE

FOUR

FIVE

SIX

SEVEN

EIGHT

NINE

Numbers 10 Thru 18

TEN

ELEVEN

TWELVE

THIRTEEN

FOURTEEN

FIFTEEN

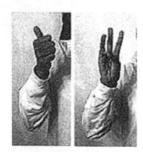

SIXTEEN

SEVENTEEN

EIGHTEEN

NUMBERS 19 THRU 23

NINETEEN

TWENTY

TWENTY ONE

TWENTY TWO

TWENTY THREE

TWENTY FOUR

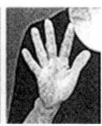

TWENTY FIVE

TWENTY SIX

TWENTY SEVEN

TWENTY EIGHT

TWENTY NINE

NUMBERS 100, 1,000, 1,000,000

ONE HUNDRED

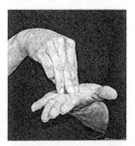

ONE THOUSAND

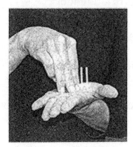

ONE MILLION

SYNTAX

American Sign Language (ASL) has a different syntax. In general, the order of our words in a sentence follows a **"TOPIC" "COMMENT"** structure.

For example:

"WEEK-PAST ME WASH CAR" or
"CAR WASH ME WEEK-PAST"

Tom Humphries and Carol Padden in their book "Learning American sign Language," indicate that there are a number of "correct" variations of word order in American Sign Language.

For example you can say:

"I STUDENT I" "I STUDENT" "STUDENT I"

All of them are correct. As far as a sentence without "be" verbs, the English sentence "I am a teacher" would be signed:

"TEACHER ME" OR "ME TEACHER"

LESSON 1

Vocabulary Words

Lesson 1

ABC's
AGAIN
DEAF / HEARING
HOW
LOVE
MEET
MISUNDERSTAND
NAME
NICE / CLEAN
PAST / FUTURE
PLEASE / SORRY
SIGN
SLOW / FAST
SPELL / FINGERSPELL
STUDENT
TEACHER
THANK YOU
UNDERSTAND
WHAT
WHEN
WHERE
WHO
WHY

Practice Sentences

Lesson 1

Do not sign words in parenthesis ().

Any word written with dashes is to be finger spelled.

1. Again please.
2. Deaf you?
3. How (are) you?
4. Love (is) nice.
5. My name (is) _____.
6. What (is) your Name?
7. Nice (to) meet you.
8. Spell your name.
9. Thank you.
10. Slow please, (I) (am) slow signing.
11. You (the) teacher?
12. Me/I student.
13. (In the) past, I/me spell my name S-u-s-i-e, now I/me spell (it) S-u-s-i.
14. (Do) you understand me?
15. You misunderstand my finger spelling?
16. Who (are) you?
17. What?
18. Where (are) you?

ALL ABOUT AMY

LESSON 1*

Amy was a young girl **who** lived with her parents in a nice house. The family would meet every morning before she went to school. She would help her mother **clean** the kitchen as **fast** as she could. She said to her mother I **love** you and out the door she went.

Amy waited for the bus to pick her up. The bus ride was always slow, and she always wondered **why**. There was a new **student** on the bus **named** Susan. They both went to the school for the **deaf.**

The teacher would meet the bus when they arrived at school. When they got to their classroom they would **finger spell** the ABC's they would do it **again** and **again**. They would have to answer questions that included **Who, What, Where, When,** and **How.**

• Words in **Bold Letters** are your vocabulary words.

NAME THAT SIGN

LESSON 1

1._____The left hand, open in the "5" position, palm up, is held before the chest. The right hand, in the right angle position, fingers pointing up, arches over and into the left palm.

2._____The right open hand is circled on the chest over the heart.

3._____The right "D: hand, with palm our and index finger straight, moves a short distance back and forth, from left to right.

4._____The right "5" hand with palm down moves from left to right, fingers wiggle

5._____Place the middle finger of the right "H" across the index of the left "H".

6._____"S" shape right hand palm in. Place on or near forehead then snap index finger up.

7._____Draw palm of right hand slowly up back of left hand, palm ddown.

8._____Right hand open palm and fingertips up. Place tips on forehead and move out into "Y" shape.

9. _____Index fingers on both hands pointing up, palms facing each other, are brought together.

10._____The right hand slowly wipes the upturned left palm from wrist to fingertips

11. _____Index fingers on both hands, palms out, index fingers tilting in, alternately rotate hands around each other..

12. _____Left "5" hand, palm up, right index finger passes over the fingers from index to little finger.

13. _____Rub the "A" hand in a circular motion over heart.

14. _____Touch the forehead with the index finger of the "V" hand and then with the middle finger of the "V" hand.

15. _____Cup both hands, palms down and knuckles touching, swing up to the palms up position, keep hands touching.

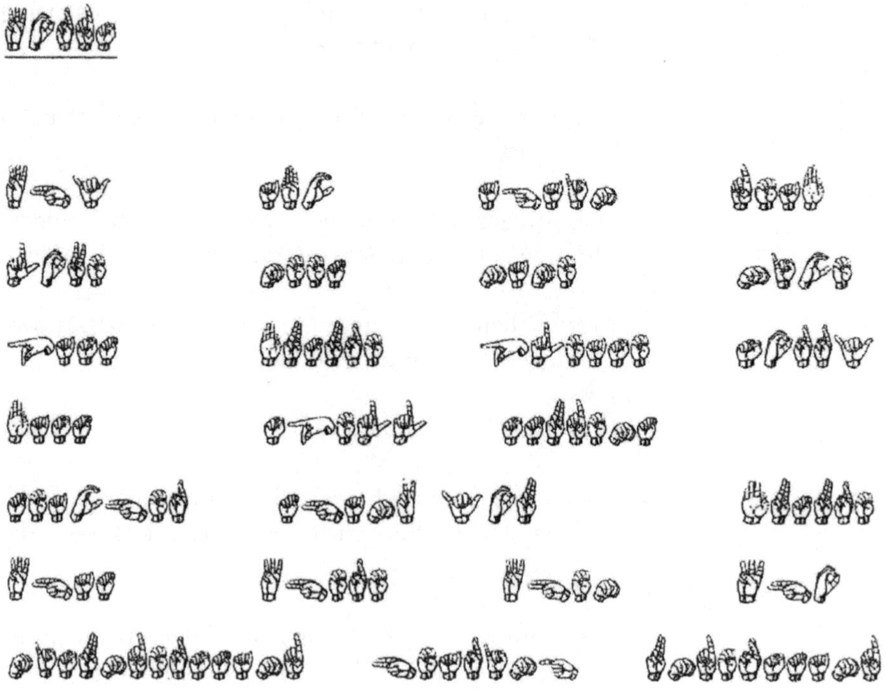

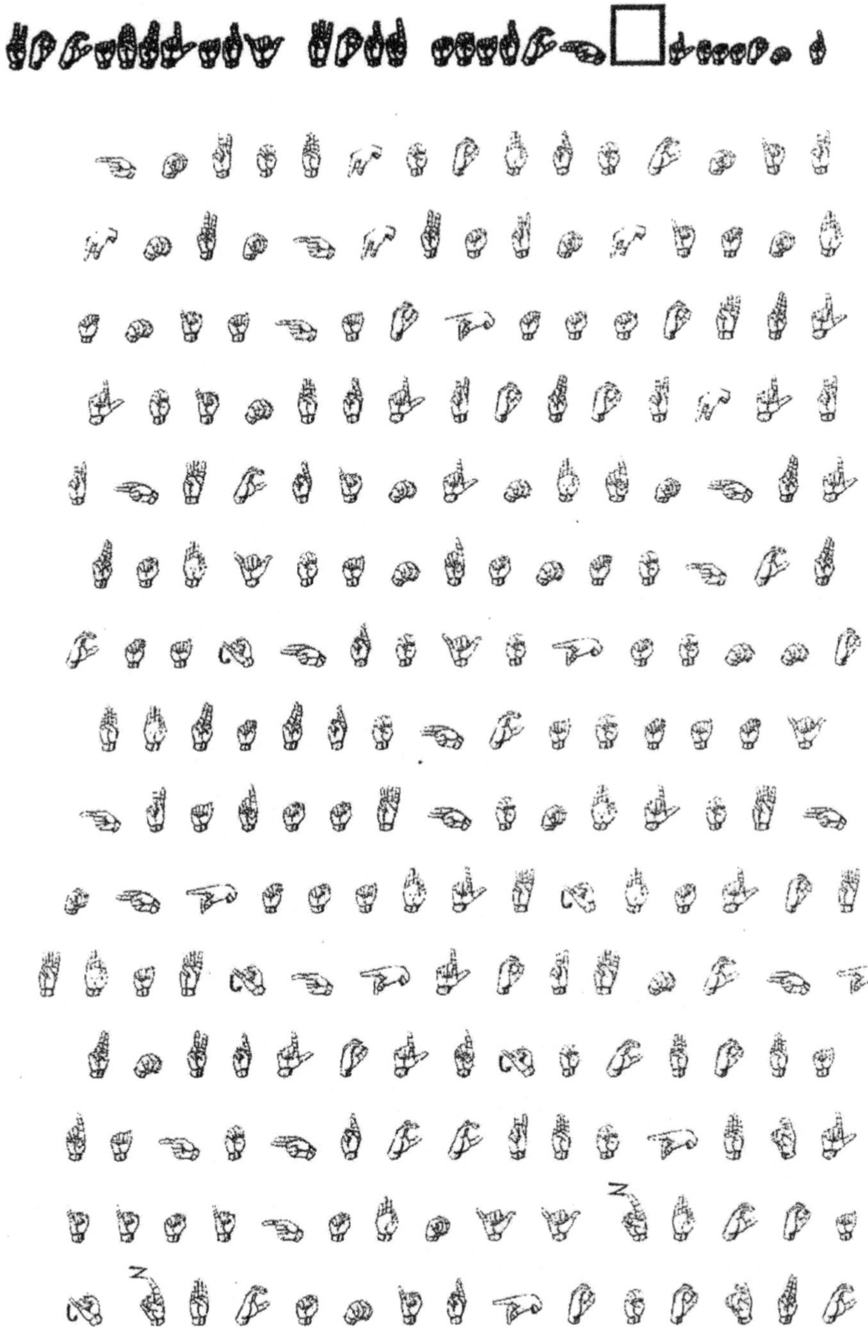

LESSON 2

Vocabulary Words

ASK / QUESTION
AUNT / UNCLE
BABY
BOOK
BOY / GIRL
BROTHER / SISTER
FAMILY
FATHER / MOTHER
FINISH / START
GOOD / BAD
HAPPY / SAD
HAVE
MAN / WOMAN
ME / YOU
MEAN
MY / MINE / YOUR
NOT / DON'T
OPEN / CLOSE
REMEMBER / FORGET
SON / DAUGHTER
TODAT / TOMORROW
WE / US
WORK

PRACTICE SENTENCES

LESSON 2

Do not sign words in parenthesis

Any word written with dashes is to be finger spelled.

1. Who (is) that (point toward person) boy?
2. My aunt (is) my mother's sister.
3. Please meet my Aunt and Uncle.
4. My mother (and) father (are in) love.
5. (That) man remembers you.
6. You forget him (points toward the person).
7. That (is a(good baby.
8. (That) boy (is) bad.
9. Please sign slower.
10. You finger spell fast.
11. Please meet my daughter (and) son.
12. I/me happy.
13. (Are) you sad?
14. I (am) finished now, you c-a-n start.
15. This (point finger out and do a sweeping arc movement) (is) my family.
16. Thank your brother (and) sister f-o-r me.
17. That (point toward couple and move ginger side to side) man (and) woman (are) brother (and) sister.
18. (It's) mine, not yours.

SARA'S FAMILY

LESSON 2[*]

Once a month Sara's **mother** and **father** would **have** a big Sunday, dinner with the **family.** They would invite their **Uncle's** and **Aunt's.** They would **start** early in the morning and **work** together all day. They all had such a **good** time.

Sara would read a **book** to her **brother, sister**, and all the other children while the other's cooked. She read stories about a **happy girl** or **boy** _who_ lived in far away places. She would read the **book** from **start** to **finish.** _When_ she **closed** the **book**, the children always wanted to hear more.

Today was a big day for the **family;** a new **baby** would join in the fun. She did not want to **forget** to **ask** the **baby's** _name._ She needed to **remember** to wash her hands before touching the baby and to talk quietly.

They all had a good time talking and eating. They all couldn't wait for the next time they would get together.

[*]   Words in **bold letters** are your vocabulary words for the week. Words that are _underlined are italicized_ are from previous lessons.

NAME THAT SIGN

LESSON 2

1._____Both "F" hands, palms facing, are held a few inches apart at chest height. They are circled around in unison so that the palms now face the body.

2._____The thumb and extended fingers of the right hand are brought up to grasp an imaginary baseball cap.

3._____The tips of the right "B" hand are placed at the lips, and then turned around and the hand is thrown down.

4._____The signer points to himself.

5._____Draw thumb of "A" hand down cheek ending in closed "D" hand shapes and index fingers side by side.

6._____Place open hands in front of you, palms facing the body. Turn suddenly so that palms face out.

7._____Touch index finger to same side of the front of the shoulder then arc to left.

8._____"B" shape both hands, palms down, tips out, index fingers touching. Arc apart, ending with palms up

9_____Both "S" hands facing down strike wrists several times.

10._____Place the open hands palm up, turn hands over palms down indexing fingers touching.

11._____The open hands pat the chest several times with a slight upward circular motion.

12._____Place the open hands palm to palm: then open them as if your opening a book. Repeat.

13._____Wipe across the forehead with the open hand, ending in the "A" position.

14._____Place the thumb of the right "A" on forehead, then drop down and touch thumb of "A" shape left hand

15._____The "5" hand is brought up against the chest.

LESSON 3

Vocabulary Words

Lesson 3

NOTES:
ALL
AND
BIG / SMALL
CAN / CAN'T
COME / GO
ENOUGH / FULL
FRIEND
GRANDMA / GRANDPA
HELP
LIKE
LIVE
MARRY / DIVORCE
NEED
NUMBER 1-23
OUT / IN
PERSON / PEOPLE
RIGHT / WRONG
SAME / DIFFERENT / BUT
SCHOOL
SEE
THAT / THIS
THINK / KNOW
WORD
YES / NO

Numbers 1 Thru 9

ONE

TWO

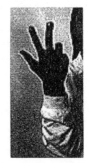

THREE

FOUR

FIVE

SIX

SEVEN

EIGHT

NINE

NUMBERS 10 THRU 18

TEN

ELEVEN

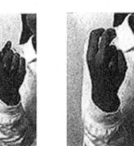
TWELVE

THIRTEEN

FOURTEEN

FIFTEEN

SIXTEEN

SEVENTEEN

EIGHTEEN

NUMBERS 19 THRU 23

NINETEEN

TWENTY

TWENTY ONE

TWENTY TWO

TWENTY THREE

Practice Sentences

Lesson 3

Do not sign words in parenthesis

Any word written with dashes is to be finger spelled.

1. All (of) my brother's and sister's help me.
2. I / Me can't go.
3. My mother (is) divorced.
4. My grandma (and) grandpa lives (in) E-m-e-r-y-v-i-l-l-e.
5. They (point index finger out and make a sweeping arc) (are the) same, not different.
6. Yes, I / Me wrong.
7. Can your daughter go (to) school?
8. I / Me (am) happy you know (the) right word.
9. ? (Do) you know your numbers?
10. Help my friend. She (index finger pointing to the side) has enough.
11. ? (Did) you see all (of the) school?
12. I/Me think (I) know (the) a-n-s-w-e-r.
13. (I) like (to be) out.
14. ? (Do) you need my help?
15. (I am) full! (you need a facial expression to make the point of being full.)
16. (It's so) big! (you need facial expressions to get the meaning with the ! mark).
17. Who s-a-i-d what, (pause a second) when, (pause a second), where, (pause), why? (you will need a facial expression for each of the WH words.)
18. And your p-o-i-n-t.

Grandma And Grandpa

Grandma and Grandpa **lived in** a **small** house **in** a **big** neighborhood. They _have_ many **friends in** the area **and** they **all** knew each other. **All** the neighbors **helped** each other **out**. **Grandma's friends** would **come** over **and** they would **go out** to eat **and** sometimes **go** shopping. **Grandma** and **Grandpa** would be _sad_ _when_ their **friends** moved **out, but** got to **know** friends _when_ others moved in.

Grandma and Grandpa grew up together and went to the **same school.** They saw each other everyday. **Grandpa liked** to carry her _books_ **home.** Grandma thought he was a very _nice boy_ **and** would grow to be a _nice man._

Grandma and Grandpa _have_ been **married** many years. **In** those years of being **married,** they raised a _son_ **and** a _daughter._ **Now** they look forward to _having_ their grandchildren **come** and visit.

---

* Words in **bold letters** are your vocabulary words. Words that are _underlined and italicized_ are from previous lessons.

NAME THAT SIGN

LESSON 3

1._____The "S" shape right hand, shake up and down at the wrist.

2._____The index finger makes a small circle on the forehead.

3._____Place the "V" shape hand in front of the face, fingertips near eyes, and move the hand outward.

4._____Place the "Y" hand in front of you palm side down and move it side to side.

5._____"P" shape on both hands, move straight down.

6._____Flat "O" shape on both hands, left palm in, right palm out, tips touching. Reverse positions twice.

7._____Clasp hands together.

8._____Place the open hand against the chest and draw away from the body, ending with the number "8" or "9."

9._____"5" shape both hands, palms facing each other. Place right thumb on chin and left thumb near edge of right hand. Move out in two jumps. (can be done with one hand.)

10._____The left hand in the "S" position. The right "5" hand, palm down. Brush several times over the top of the left hand.

11._____Move both "S" hands downward in a firm manner.

12._____Both palms down the right index strikes the tip of the left index finger and passes it in a downward movement.

13._____The right hand is in a "5" shape, palm in, tips facing left. Move from left to right, closing into flat O.

14._____The index "X" shape fingers are interlocked with each other. They Separate, change their relative positions and come together again.

15._____The hands are clapped together several times.

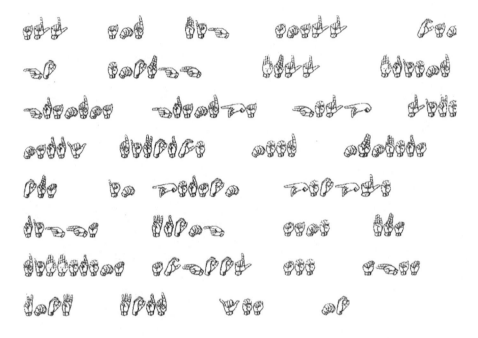

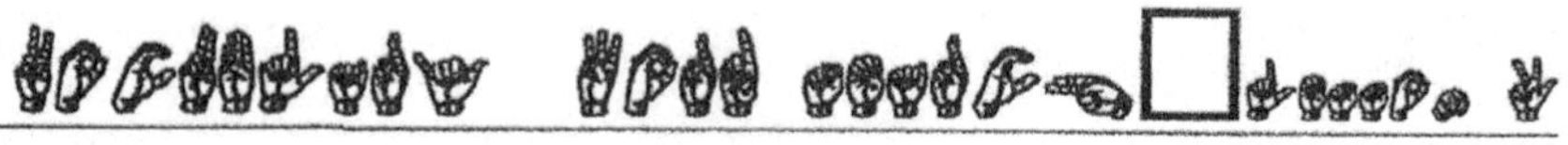

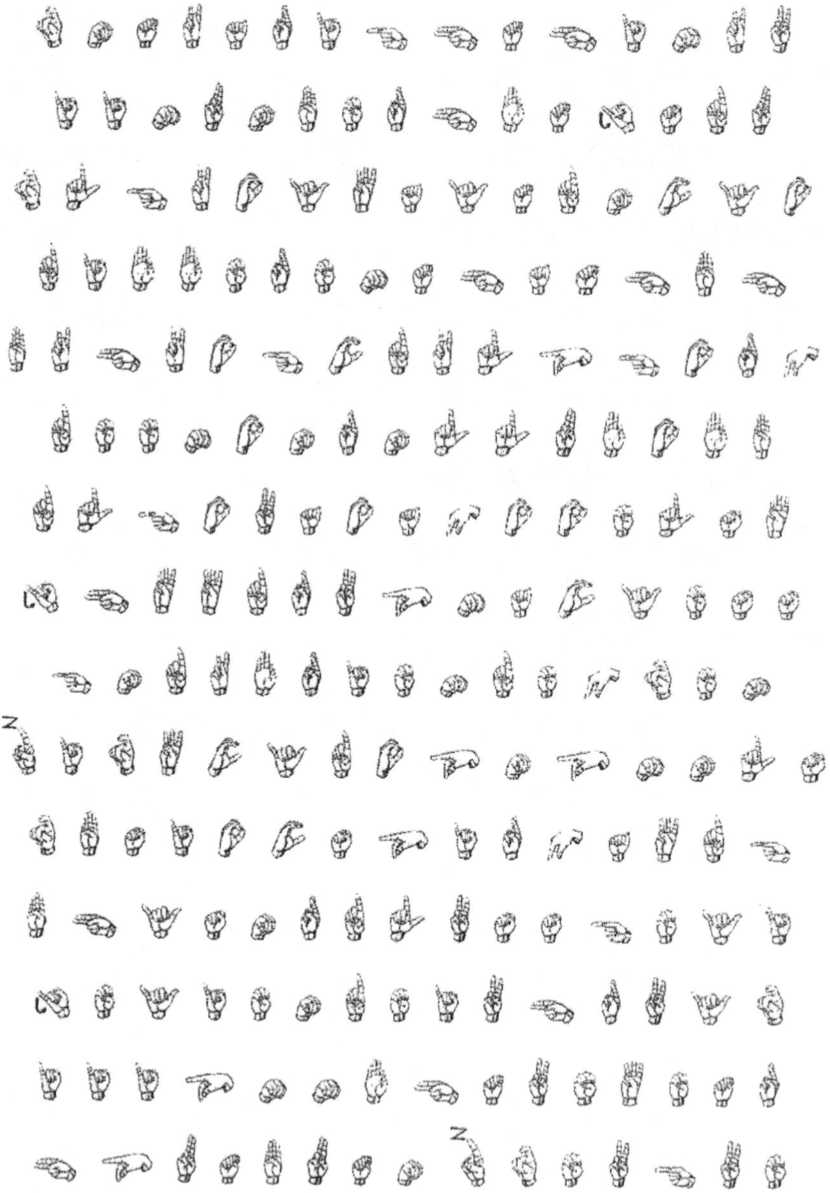

LESSON 4

Vocabulary Words

Lesson 4

NOTES:
ANGRY / MAD
BATHROOM / TOILET
CHILDREN / CHILD
COMPUTER
FEEL
FINE
FOOD / EAT
HERE
HOME
HOUR / TIME
HOUSE
MILK
MONTH
MORNING / NIGHT
NOW
OLD / NEW
SIT / STAND
STAY / LEAVE
TREE
WATER
WEEK
YESTERDAY

Practice Sentences

Lesson 4

Do not sign words in parenthesis

Any word written with dashes is to be finger spelled.

1. ? (Are) angry you?
2. I / Me need (to) go (to) (the) bathroom.
3. Help me w-i-t-h (the) computer.
4. I / Me feel fine. (pause a second) How (are) you?
5. (Do) you have milk (in) your house?
6. 1 year f-r-o-m today, this month, my son will (be) home.
7. Please, you can't leave. Stay (and) have (something to) eat.
8. (The) bathroom (is) (to the) right.
9. (What) time (of the) morning, (do we) leave?
10. Good night.
11. Standup, don't sit.
12. Last week (we) went (to the) p-a-r-k.
13. Who went (to the) p-a-r-k w-i-t-h you?
14. My, mother, brother, father, sister, aunt, and uncle all went (to the) p-a-r-k w-i-t-h me.
15. That school (is) old. (The) new school (is) (on the) left.
16. (The) new school address (use the sign "live" with an "a" hand shape) (is) 1-2-3-4.
17. What hour (do) (we) meet your mother (and) father?
18. My sister will (get) married next week.

TROUBLE WITH THE TOILET

LESSON 4[*]

Mom and dad were *having* trouble with their **computer** *and* *needed* to *have* it fixed. They told the **children** they would be **leaving** in a few minutes *and* be gone for a few **hours** *that* **morning.** The **children** were **old** enough to **stay** alone. *Mom* was still a little nervous to **leave** them *but* *dad* said it was ok. They put the **computer** *in* the car along with some **food** they were going to drop off at a *friend's* **house.**

Dad received a call from their *son* about an **hour** later telling him *that* the **toilet** *in* the **bathroom** was overflowing *and* the **water** was going everywhere. His *son* thought *dad* would be **mad** *but* he was *not.* *Dad* was very calm *and* told his *son* *how* to **close** off the **water.** The **toilet** would be **fine** *and* he would fix it *when* he got **home.**

When *dad* came **home** he fixed the problem *and* told his *son* he did a *good* job *and* **now** he *knew* *what* to do the next **time** it happened.

---

[*]   Words in **bold letters** are your vocabulary words. Words that are *underlined and italicized* are from previous lessons.

NAME THAT SIGN

LESSON 4

1._____Form "claw" hand shape in front of the face open and close fingers a few times.

2._____Shake the "T" hand from left to right several times.

3._____The thumb of the "C" hand taps the forehead.

4._____The thumb tip of the "A" or "Y" hand rests on the right chin. It then moves back a short distance.

5._____The tip of the index finger of the "W" hand touches the lips a number of times.

6._____The upright closed "D" hand is placed palm to palm against the left "5" hand palm up. The right "D" hand moves along the left palm to fingertips.

7._____Rotate the right closed "D" hand in a circle on the left open hand.

8._____Move both flat hands, palms up, in opposite forward circles in front of the body.

9._____Place the right "S" hand under chin then move down in a wavy motion.

10._____The "5" shape of the hand, place the thumb on the chest and, tap the chest a few times.

11._____"5" hand middle finger strikes upward on chest.

12._____Squeeze the "S" hands a few times.

13._____The left index finger is held up palm right. The right index is moved from the tip of the left finger down to the knuckle chest side.

14._____Place both bent hands before you, palms up. Drop the hands slightly. Sometimes made with the "Y" hands instead the bent hands.

15._____Stand the "V" fingers of one hand on the flat of palm of the other hand.

LESSON 5

Vocabulary Words

Lesson 5

NOTES:

ANY / OTHER
BED / SLEEP
BLACK
BLUE
BROWN
COLOR
DRINK
DRIVE
EXCUSE
GOLD
GREEN
MAKE
MOVE / PUT
ORANGE
PHONE
PINK
PURPLE
RED
SHOP / STORE
SILVER
TALK
WAIT
WHITE
YELLOW

PRACTICE SENTENCES

LESSON 5

Do not sign words in parenthesis

Any word written with dashes is to be finger spelled.

1. ? (Are there) any other bathrooms I / Me can use?
2. Go (to) bed, (it is) time (to) sleep.
3. Don't drink (and) drive.
4. My brother (is) making excuses (for) last night.
5. What color (is) that house?
6. Wait, please I / Me want (to) go with you.
7. Can you move gold coat?
8. ? Does (the) red lipstick look ok?
9. Who wants (to) talk (to) me (on) (the) phone?
10. (The) store (is) pink outside and white inside.
11. What color (do) you like?
12. I / Me like black and purple.
13. Some yellows look orange.
14. (The) fox (is) brown.
15. Put (the) blue b-o-w-l on (the) computer.
16. Can I / Me drink out (of) (the) silver cup?
17. My daughter's friend (has) green h-a-i-r.
18. Good night, sleep good.

NAME THAT SIGN

LESSON 5

1._____Move the right fingertips over the lower part of the left flat hand a few times.

2._____The tip of the right index finger moves down across the lips. The "R" hand may also be used.

3._____Hold the right extended "A" hand with palm in, swing down in an arc.

4._____The right "Y" hand is placed at the right side of the head with the thumb touching the ear and the little finger touching the lips.

5._____The flat "O" shape both hands, tips down. Swing out twice.

6._____Hold both hands, palm up, one hand slightly ahead of the other. Wiggle the fingers of both hands.

7._____Shake the right "G" hand, in front of body.

8._____"B" hand touches lips several times, (open fingers).

9._____Place the "5" hand in front of the chin and wiggle the fingers.

10._____Make two "S" hands like steering a car.

11._____Touch the right ear with the right index finger. Move the right "Y" hand down and forward and shake it.

12._____Hold the fingertips of the right curved open hand on the chest and move it forward as it closes to an "and" hand.

13._____"S" hands, palms facing, place one "S" hand on top of the other, twist and touch several times.

14._____The down turned flat "O" hands, move together from left to right, in an arc.

15._____Move the right "B" hand index finger down the right cheek.

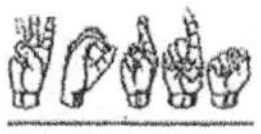

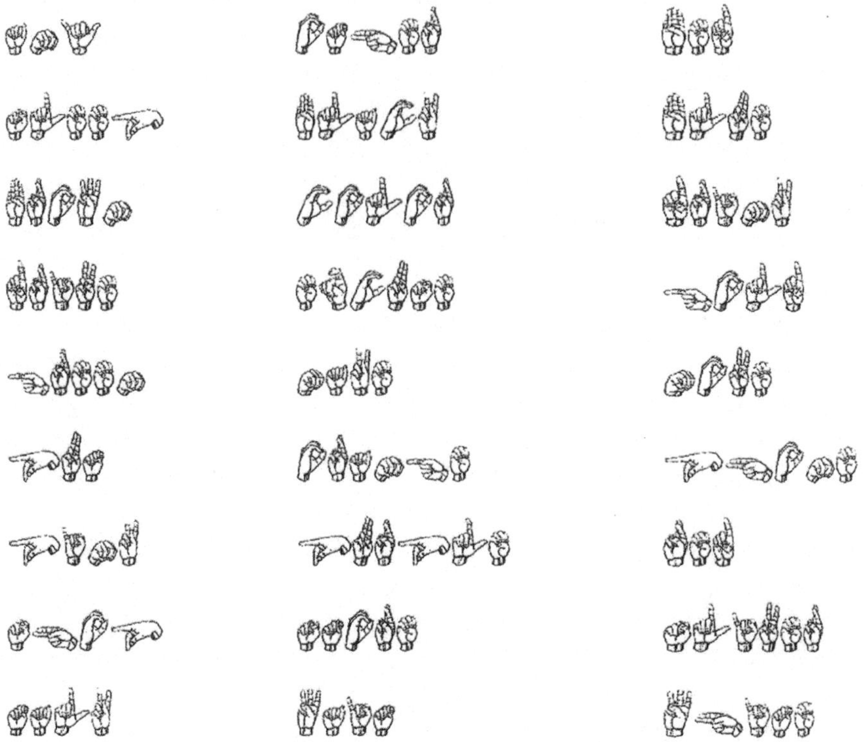

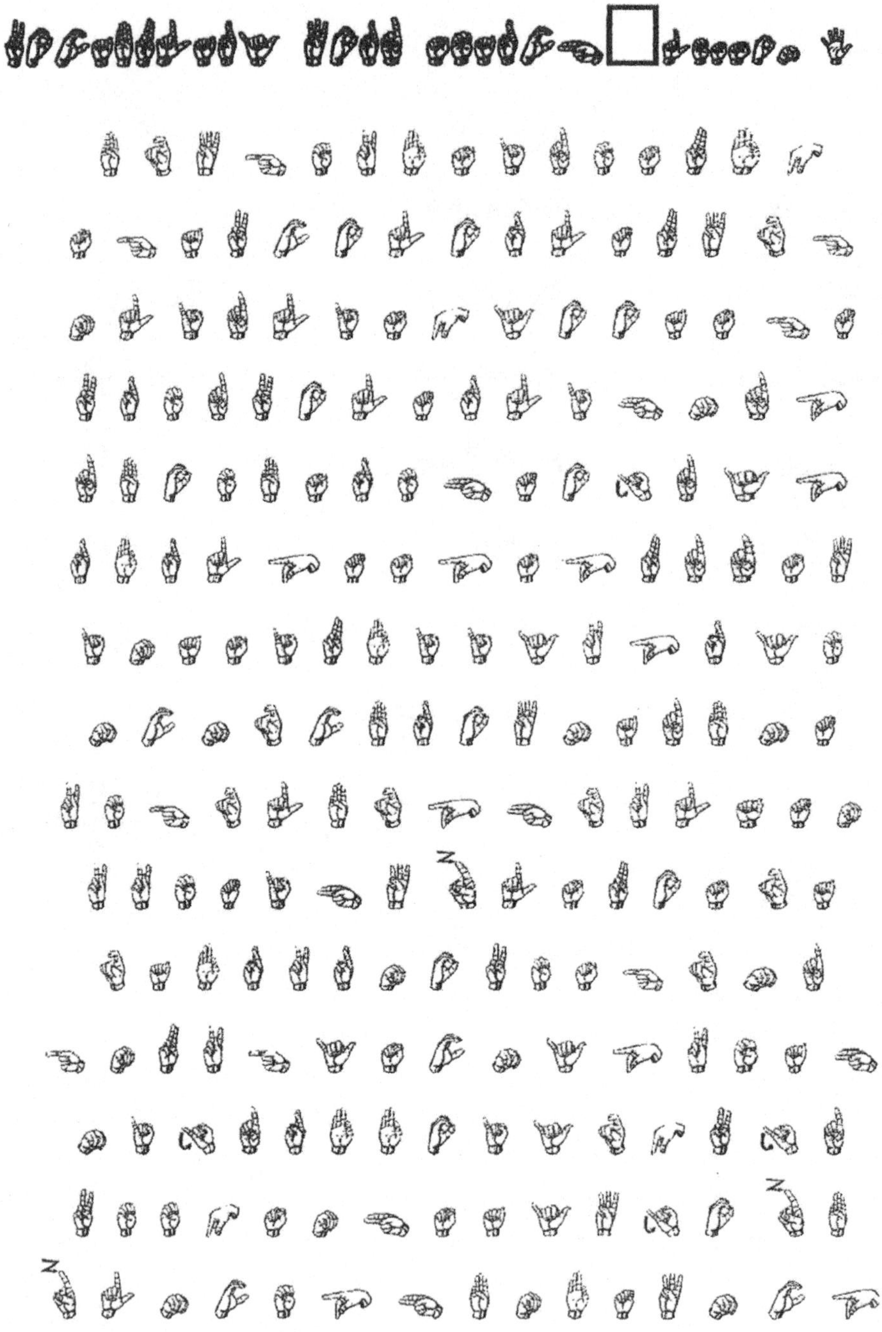

LESSON 6

VOCABULARY WORDS

LESSON 6

NOTES:

BEFORE / AFTER
COAT
COFFEE / TEA
DO
DOG / CAT / BIRD
FLOWER
FOR
GET
GIVE
HAPPEN
LIGHT / DARK
LISTEN
NEAR / FAR
NUMBERS 24 – 100, 1,000, 1,000,000
READY
SOCKS / SHOES
TALL / SMALL
TRY
WANT / DON'T WANT
WITH / WITHOUT

NUMBERS 24 THRU 29

TWENTY FOUR

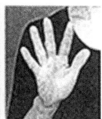

TWENTY FIVE

TWENTY SIX

TWENTY SEVEN

TWENTY EIGHT

TWENTY NINE

Numbers 44 And 49

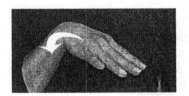

FORTY FOUR

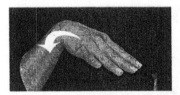

FORTY NINE

NUMBERS 100, 1,000, 1,000,000

ONE HUNDRED

ONE THOUSAND

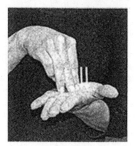

ONE MILLION

PRACTICE SENTENCES

LESSON 6

Do not sign words in parenthesis

Any word written with dashes is to be finger spelled.

1. I / Me can hear (a) dog (and) cat fighting.
2. ? (Is it) light (or) dark outside, which?
3. Please close that door.
4. Where (are) your socks (and) shoes?
5. With (or) without (the) car, I / Me don't want (to) go!
6. What happened?
7. (Did) you have coffee, before (or) after (the) class?
8. That (is) (a) pretty flower.
9. What (is) (the) word for this sign?
10. Give me some water.
11. You need (to) try (a) little harder.
12. ? (Are) you ready?
13. Josh lives near here.
14. He (is a) tall man.
15. Get ready (so) we can leave (on) time.

CHOOSING COLORS

LESSON 5 & 6*

Katie **wanted** to _go_ back to **bed** _and_ **sleep,** she was tired from the _night_ **before. Any other** day Katie knew she could use _that_ as an **excuse.** _But today_ she had _work_ to do _and needed_ to _finish._

She **drank** her **coffee, put** on her **socks** _and_ **shoes** to _start_ her morning; _now_ she was **ready for** the day. She _needed_ to **make** a few **phone** calls to **talk** about some things **before driving** to the **store.**

The **shop** she _needed_ to _go_ to wasn't _that_ **far** from her _house._ It was a **small flower shop** on the **other** side of town. **With** the list she had made from _yesterday_, she _knew what_ to **get,** and **tried** _not to forget_ anything.

While looking **for** _different_ **color flowers** and paper she _needed_ to cover the tables, it **happened** she came up **with** an idea **for** some new things to **do.**

As she walked around picking _out different_ **colored flowers** in **red, pink, yellow, blue** and **orange,** she _knew_ she had to **put** some **green** leaves _in_ with them. **After** _that_ she went to look **for** the paper she _needed._ Looking over the **silver** and **gold,** she decided to go **with** the **gold** and **white.**

After waiting _in_ line she _remembered_ she _needed_ **number** cards to **put** on the tables to **give** the people an idea _where_ they should _sit._

Katie **put** _all_ the things _in_ her car; she was _finished_ **with** her **shopping.**

---

*   Words in **bold letters** are your vocabulary words. Words that are _underlined and italic_ are from previous lessons.

NAME THAT SIGN

LESSON 6

1._____The index fingers, palms down, pointing forward are rubbed back and forth against each other.

2._____Both open "B" hands, palms toward body, thumbs up. Place the right hand against left palm then move right hand towards body.

3._____Hold both "claw" hands with palms up. Move both hands towards the body.

4._____Point both index fingers palm up, and then turn palms down. (can also be done with the "H" hands)

5._____The "R" hands are held side by side, with palms facing down, they move in opposite directions at the same time

6._____Place the tips of the "And" hand shape first under one nostril, then under the other.

7._____Both "S" shape hands, palms facing chest, turn hands so palms face down. (can be done with "T" hands also)

8._____Both "And" hands held before the chest and then moved outward in an arc, away from the body.

9._____Place the "A" hands together, palm to palm.

10._____Slap the right hand on the right leg and snap the finger.

11._____The right hand is placed, usually slightly cupped, behind the right ear. (can be done with the "L" hand also).

12._____Slide the right closed "D" index finger up palm of left hand.

13._____Point toward the forehead with the closed "D" shape index finger; then slide forward ending with the index finger pointing forward

14._____The right "S" hand, palm facing left, rotates in a counterclockwise manner atop the left "S" hand, palm facing right.

15._____Move both down turned "C" hands in unison to the left then to the right.

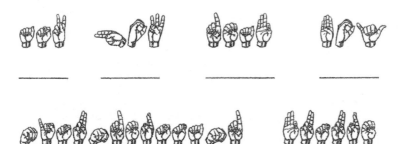

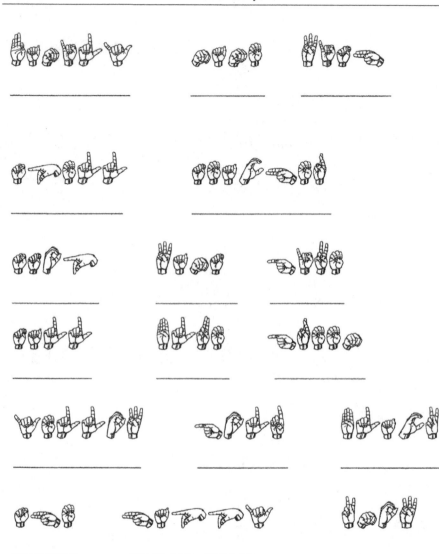

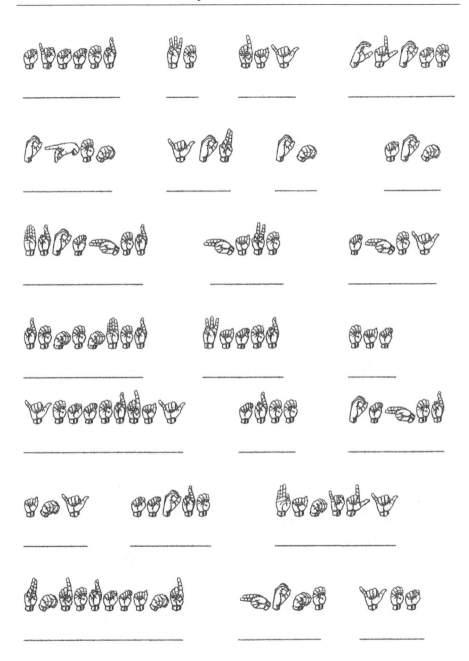

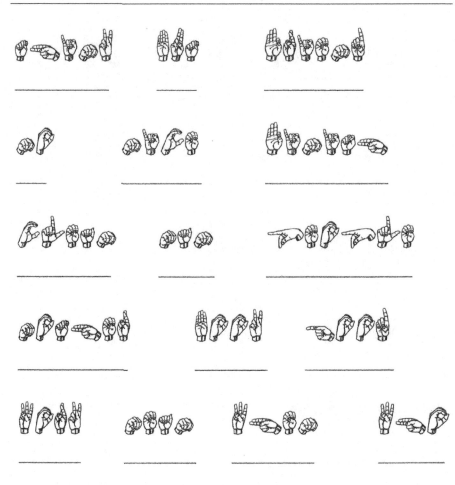

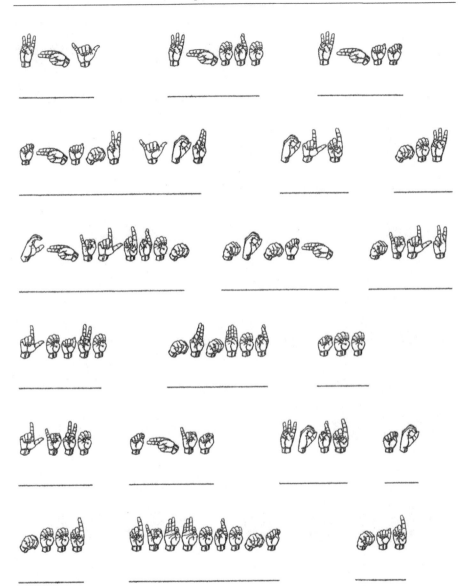

_____   _____   _____

_____   _____   _____

_____   _____   _____

_____   _____   _____   _____

_____   _____   _____

_____   _____

_____   _____   _____

_____   _____   _____

_____   _____   _____

_____   _____   _____

ANSWERS

VOCABULARY WORD SEARCH SOLUTION

LESSON 1

```
G  ★  ★  E  ★  ★  E  ★  ★  ★  ★  ★  M  ★  ★
★  N  ★  M  ★  ★  V  S  ★  ★  ★  I  ★  ★  ★
★  N  I  A  G  A  O  ★  T  ★  S  ★  ★  ★  ★
★  ★  I  N  B  R  L  K  ★  U  ★  ★  ★  ★  ★
★  ★  ★  C  R  ★  N  ★  N  ★  D  M  ★  ★  ★
★  ★  ★  Y  E  A  ★  D  S  N  ★  E  ★  ★  U
★  ★  ★  ★  H  R  E  ★  E  P  S  E  N  ★  O
★  F  U  T  U  R  E  H  C  A  E  T  A  T  Y
★  ★  A  ★  S  ★  W  H  E  ★  F  L  E  W  H
★  H  ★  T  S  A  F  L  W  ★  ★  S  L  O  W
W  ★  A  ★  ★  ★  P  ★  ★  ★  ★  ★  C  H  ★
★  N  ★  ★  ★  ★  ★  ★  ★  ★  ★  O  ★  ★
D  ★  G  ★  ★  ★  ★  ★  ★  ★  ★  ★  ★  ★  ★
★  ★  ★  I  ★  ★  ★  ★  ★  ★  ★  ★  ★  ★  ★
★  ★  ★  ★  S  ★  ★  ★  ★  ★  ★  ★  ★  ★  ★
```

ABC'S
AGAIN
DEAF / HEARING
HOW
LOVE
MEET
MISUNDERSTAND
NAME
NICE / CLEAN
PAST / FUTURE
PLEASE / SORRY
SIGN

SLOW / FAST
SPELL
STUDENT
TEACHER
THANK YOU
UNDERSTAND
WHAT
WHEN
WHERE
WHO
WHY

VOCABULARY WORD SEARCH SOLUTION

LESSON 3

```
★  ★  T  ★  ★  R  I  G  H  T  H  I  N  K  ★
★  I  N  U  M  B  E  R  ★  ★  ★  ★  S  ★  ★
★  L  G  ★  O  ★  W  A  ★  ★  ★  M  C  ★  ★
D  I  F  F  E  R  E  N  T  H  A  T  H  ★  ★
B  K  ★  K  O  G  C  D  ★  L  ★  G  O  ★  ★
D  E  E  N  ★  M  R  M  L  L  U  F  O  ★  ★
★  ★  G  O  ★  A  ★  A  ★  O  ★  ★  L  ★  ★
★  ★  ★  W  ★  R  V  P  N  A  C  Y  E  S  ★
★  ★  ★  ★  F  R  I  E  N  D  ★  ★  ★  E  ★
★  ★  ★  W  C  Y  D  O  ★  ★  P  ★  M  ★  S
★  ★  ★  ★  O  ★  S  P  ★  ★  ★  A  W  D  G
★  ★  ★  ★  M  R  ★  L  ★  S  S  ★  E  Y  I
★  ★  ★  ★  E  ★  D  E  I  ★  ★  ★  ★  ★  ★
★  ★  ★  P  ★  ★  ★  H  ★  V  ★  ★  ★  ★  ★
★  ★  ★  ★  B  U  T  ★  ★  ★  E  ★  ★  ★  ★
```

ALL	OUT
SMALL	PEOPLE
GO	SAME
FRIEND	SCHOOL
HELP	THIS
MARRY	WORD
NUMBERS	BIG
PERSON	COME
WRONG	FULL
DIFFERENT	GRANDPA
THAT	LIVE
KNOW	NEED
NO	IN
AND	RIGHT
CAN	BUT
ENOUGH	SEE
GRANDMA	THINK
LIKE	YES
DIVORCE	

VOCABULARY WORD SEARCH SOLUTION

LESSON 5

```
★  ★  ★  ★  E  ★  ★  S  ★  ★  ★  S  ★  ★  ★
S  ★  ★  V  C  O  L  O  R  ★  T  ★  W  ★  ★
★  L  I  D  ★  I  ★  ★  ★  O  ★  A  S  ★  ★
★  R  E  D  V  ★  ★  ★  R  ★  I  H  N  ★  ★
D  B  O  E  B  ★  R  E  H  T  O  ★  ★  Y  ★
R  ★  R  L  P  ★  S  P  ★  P  U  ★  ★  ★  ★
I  ★  A  ★  ★  U  ★  ★  I  ★  ★  P  ★  ★  ★
N  C  N  ★  C  B  R  O  W  N  ★  D  B  ★  ★
K  E  G  X  ★  ★  ★  P  ★  ★  K  L  A  T  ★
★  K  E  T  I  H  W  ★  L  ★  U  O  ★  ★  ★
★  A  ★  R  ★  ★  M  O  V  E  ★  G  ★  ★  ★
★  M  ★  ★  G  ★  ★  ★  N  ★  ★  ★  ★  ★  ★
★  ★  ★  ★  ★  ★  ★  O  ★  ★  ★  ★  ★  ★  ★
★  ★  ★  ★  ★  ★  H  ★  ★  ★  ★  ★  ★  ★  ★
★  ★  ★  ★  ★  P  ★  ★  ★  ★  ★  ★  ★  ★  ★
```

ANY
BLUE
DRINK
GOLD
MOVE
PHONE
PUT
SLEEP
TALK
BED
BROWN
DRIVE
GREEN
ORANGE

PINK
RED
SLIVER
WAIT
BLACK
COLOR
EXCUSE
MAKE
OTHER
PURPLE
SHOP
STORE
WHITE

NAME THAT SIGN

ANSWER SHEET

Lesson 1	Lesson 2	Lesson 3	Lesson 4	Lesson 5	Lesson 6
1. again	1. family	1. yes	1. mad	1. excuse	1. socks
2. please	2. boy	2. think	2. toilet	2. red	2. before
3. where	3. bad	3. see	3. computer	3. any	3. want
4. finger spell	4. me	4. same	4. yesterday	4. phone	4. happen
5. name	5. sister	5. person	5. water	5. store/shop	5. ready
6. understand	6. finish	6. number	6. week	6. wait	6. flower
7. slow	7. we	7. married	7. hour	7. green	7. try
8. why	8. open	8. like	8. hear	8. talk	8. give
9. meet	9. work	9. grandma	9. old	9. color	9. with
10. nice	10. closed	10. enough	10. fine	10. drive	10. dog
11. sign	11. happy	11. can	11. feel	11. gold	11. listen
12. what	12. book	12. can't	12. milk	12. white	12. tall
13. sorry	13. forget	13. and	13. month	13. make	13. for
14. misunderstand	14. remember	14. friend	14. now	14. put	14. coffee
15. how	15. mine	15. school	15. stand	15. brown	15. do

LESSON 6 TEST ANSWERS

AGAIN, AUNT, DEAF, HOW, BOOK, GIRL, LOVE, CAN, COMPUTER, MEET, MISUNDERSTAND, NAME, CLEAN, PLEASE, THANK YOU, UNDERSTAND, WHERE, HOW YOU, WHAT YOUR NAME, YOU TEACHER, YOU MISUNDERSTAND MY FINGER SPELLING, NICE MEET YOU, WHY, BROTHER, SON, MEAN, GOOD, REMEMBER, WORK, TOMORROW, WHO THAT BOY, PLEASE MEET MY AUNT AND UNCLE, THAT GOOD BABY, YOU SAD, PLEASE SIGN SLOWER, OPEN, HAPPY, MOTHER, UNCLE, WOMAN, NOT, START, SISTER, ALL, BIG, ENOUGH, YES, LIVE, HELP, LIKE, PERSON, DIFFERENT, MARRY, THINK, GRANDPA, WRONG, FRIEND, GO, SEE, WORD, I CAN'T GO, I HAPPY YOU KNOW RIGHT WORD, YOU NEED MY HELP, YES I WRONG, HELP MY FRIEND, ANGRY, FOOD, FEEL, YESTERDAY, OLD, NOW, WEEK, MORNING, HOUSE, HOUR, MILK, ANGRY YOU, I FEEL FINE HOW YOU, YOU HAVE MILK, YOUR HOUSE, GOOD NIGHT, MY SISTER WILL MARRY NEXT WEEK, ANY, BLACK, BLUE, MAKE, MOVE, RED, PURPLE, TALK, WAIT, EXCUSE, COLOR, DON'T DRINK AND DRIVE, WHAT COLOR THAT HOUSE, WHAT COLOR YOU LIKE, GOOD NIGHT SLEEP GOOD, SOME YELLOWS LOOK ORANGE.

VOCABULARY WORD PICTURES LESSONS 1 THRU 6

Again

Deaf

Hearing

How

Love

Meet

Misunderstand

Name

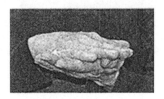

Nice / Clean

Past

  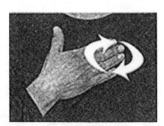

Future Please

Sorry Sign

Slow Fast

Spell / Finger Spell

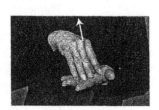  

Student

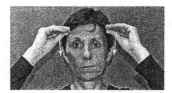

Teacher

Thank You

Understand

What

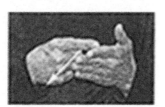 

What

When

Where

Who

Who

Why

Ask

Question

Aunt

Uncle

Baby

Book

Boy

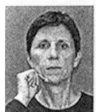 

Girl

Brother

Sister

Family

Father

Mother

Finish

Start

Good

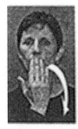

Bad

Happy

Don't

Open   Closed

Remember   Forget

Son

Daughter

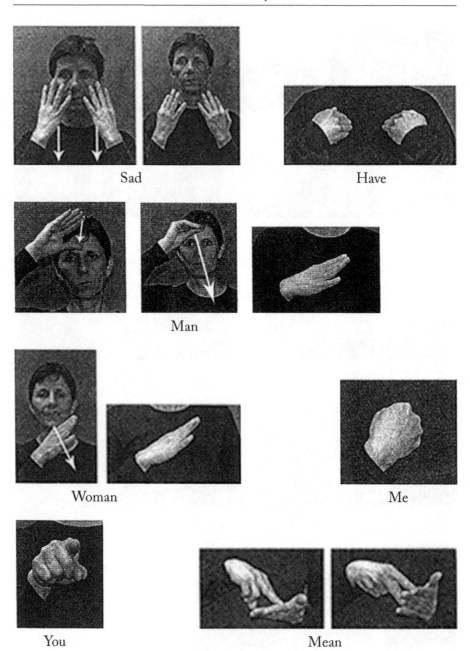

Sad

Have

Man

Woman

Me

You

Mean

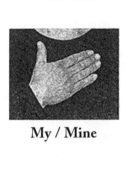

My / Mine

Your

Not

Today

Tomorrow

We

 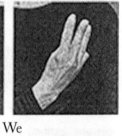

We

Us

Work

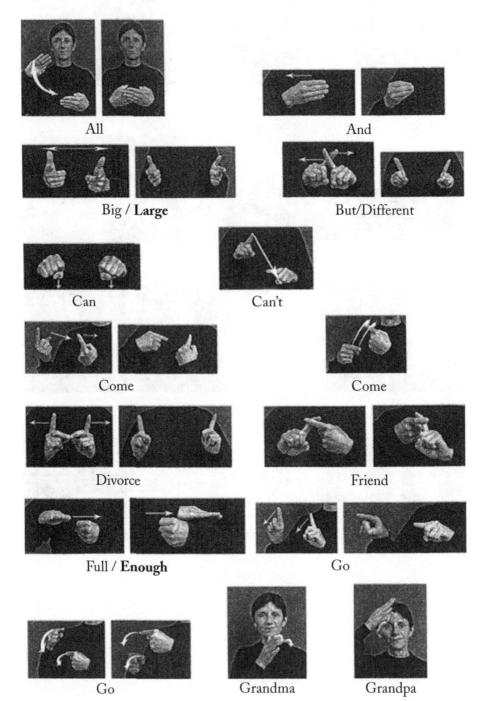

All

And

Big / **Large**

But/Different

Can

Can't

Come

Come

Divorce

Friend

Full / **Enough**

Go

Go

Grandma

Grandpa

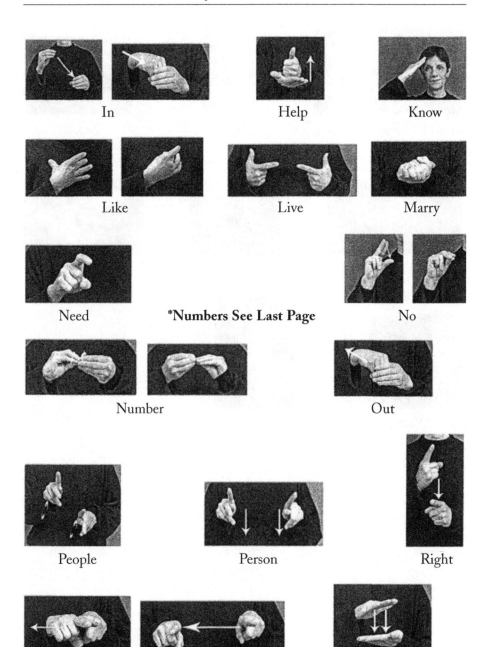

In

Help

Know

Like

Live

Marry

Need

*Numbers See Last Page

No

Number

Out

People

Person

Right

Same

School

See

Small

Small

That

Think

This

Wrong

Yes

NUMBERS:

One · Two · Three · Four

Five · Six · Seven · Eight

Nine · Ten · Eleven · Twelve

Thirteen · Fourteen · Fifteen · Sixteen

Seventeen · Eighteen · Nineteen

Twenty · Twenty One · Twenty Two

Twenty Three

Angry / Mad

Bathroom / Restroom **Children**

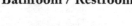

Child **Computer**

Feel Fine Food / Eat

Here Home

Hour

 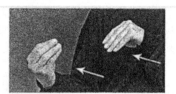

Leave

Toilet   **Tree**   **Water**

 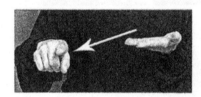

Week

Yesterday

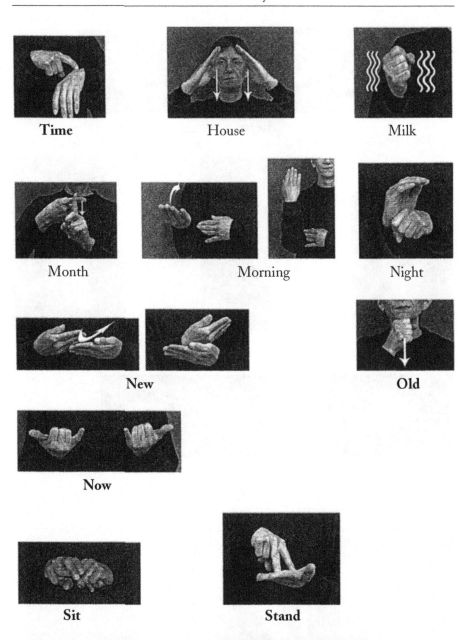

Time   House   Milk

Month   Morning   Night

New   Old

Now

Sit   **Stand**

Stay

Any

Other

Bed

Black

Blue

Brown

Color

Drink

Drive

Excuse

Gold

Green

Make

Orange

Phone

Pink

Purple

Put

Red

Silver

Sleep

Shop / Store

Talk

Talk

Wait

White

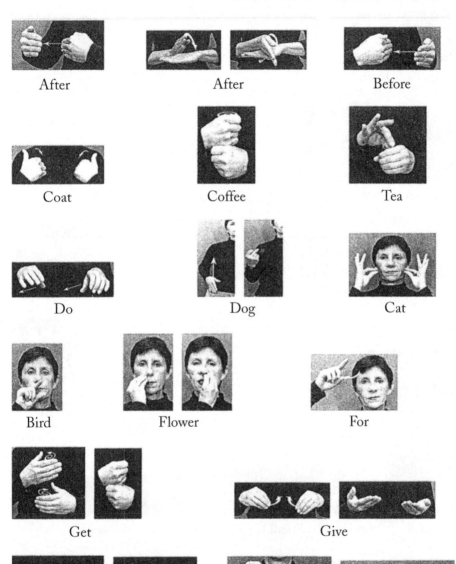

After

After

Before

Coat

Coffee

Tea

Do

Dog

Cat

Bird

Flower

For

Get

Give

Happen

Light

Dark

Listen

Near

Far

*(Numbers see last page)

Ready

Socks

Shoes

Tall

Tall

Small

Small

Try

Want

Don't Want

With

Without

NUMBERS:

Twenty Four

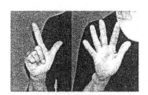

Twenty Five

Twenty Six

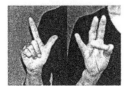

Twenty Seven

Twenty Eight

Twenty Nine

Forty Four

Forty Nine

One Hundred

One Thousand

One Million